MARIO LEMIEUX

OWN THE ICE

BY
MARK STEWART

THE MILLBROOK PRESS
BROOKFIELD, CONNECTICUT

M

THE MILLBROOK PRESS

Produced by
BITTERSWEET PUBLISHING,
John Sammis, President
and
TEAM STEWART, INC.
Researched and Edited by Mike Kennedy

Design and Electronic Page Makeup by
JAFFE ENTERPRISE, Ron Jaffe

All photos courtesy AP/ Wide World Photos, Inc. except the following:
Doug Pensinger/ALLSPORT — Front Cover
Brian Bahr/ALLSPORT — Back Cover
St. Louis Blues — Page 9 top
The following images are from the collection of Team Stewart:
Sports Illustrated for Kids/TIME INC © 1996 — Page 9 bottom
Classic Games, Inc. ©1992 — Page 10
The Hockey News © 1982 — Page 11 top
Topps Chewing Gum, Inc. © 1972 — Page 13 top
Topps Chewing Company, Inc. © 1976 — Page 13 bottom
The National Hockey League © 1985 — Page 20
The Hockey News © 1987 — Page 27 top
O-Pee-Chee Co. Ltd. © 1989 — Page 27 bottom
O-Pee-Chee Co. Ltd. © 1991 — Page 33
The National Hockey League © 1992 — Page 42

Printed in the United States of America

Published by
The Millbrook Press, Inc.
2 Old New Milford Road
Brookfield, Connecticut 06804

www.millbrookpress.com

Library of Congress Cataloging-in-Publication Data

Stewart, Mark.
  Mario Lemieux : own the ice / by Mark Stewart.
    p. cm.
Includes index.
Summary: A biography of the hockey superstar who overcame injury, disease,
and even aging to return to the rink.
  ISBN 0-7613-2555-7 (lib. bdg.)   ISBN 0-7613-1687-6 (pbk.)
  1. Lemieux, Mario, 1965– —Juvenile literature. 2. Hockey players—
Canada—Biography—Juvenile literature. [1. Lemieux, Mario,1965– 2. Hockey
players.] I. Title.
  GV848.5.L46 S84 2002
  796.962'092—dc21
                                                              2001007006

          1 3 5 7 9 10 8 6 4 2   (lib. bdg.)
          1 3 5 7 9 10 8 6 4 2   (pbk.)

CONTENTS

NATIONAL OBSESSION

1

"He didn't have a kid's attitude."

CHILDHOOD FRIEND MARC BERGEVIN

You do *not* turn the channel when *Hockey Night in Canada* is on TV. It is a national obsession. A certain baby-sitter learned this lesson the hard way one evening in 1973. She made the mistake of telling 8-year-old Mario Lemieux and his brothers, Richard and Alain, that she wanted to watch a movie instead of the game. After they locked her in the bathroom, the boys turned up the volume to drown out her screams.

Three decades later, Mario is still obsessed with hockey. Regardless of the obstacles he has encountered, the Pittsburgh Penguins' superstar has always found a way to immerse himself in the sport. No one in history has gone through more to play the game he loves. Some say no one has ever played the game better.

Mario was born on October 5, 1965. His father, Jean-Guy, was a construction worker. His mother, Pierette, was what

DID YOU KNOW?

In French, "Le Mieux" means "The Best."

some call a "hockey mom." She took care of her three boys, and chauffeured them to

Mario acknowledges the cheers of the Pittsburgh Penguins' fans.
He has been hearing hockey crowds roar since he was nine years old.

The historic Montreal Forum, where Mario dreamed of playing one day.

practices and games. The Lemieux family lived in Ville Emard, just outside of the French-speaking city of Montreal.

Mario got his first pair of skates as soon as he learned to walk. He joined Richard and Alain on the ice, pushing a small chair before him for balance. As children, the Lemieux boys did most of their skating at a rink behind a nearby church. The place they *really* wanted to skate was the Forum, where the Montreal Canadiens played. Six times between 1971 and 1979, the team won the Stanley Cup, which is awarded to the National Hockey League's annual champion. "Growing up in Montreal, you want to be a hockey player," says Mario. "You see the Canadiens win all those Stanley Cups. My goal was to do that one year."

Mario's favorite player was Guy Lafleur, an electrifying skater and artistic goal-scorer. He was the star of the Canadiens, a team packed with great performers. The

Guy Lafleur (left) cut a dashing figure on the ice. Mario idolized him.

"Mario brings a creativity to the game that a lot of us strive for. He's had it from day one."

MIKE MODANO
(LEFT)

Canadiens won because they were always thinking two steps ahead, and played excellent team defense. Every kid growing up in French Canada knew that this was the secret of Montreal's success. But only a handful of young players could actually play this way.

Mario was one of those kids. He skated with power and confidence, he directed crisp passes to teammates, and he could anticipate where the "holes" would be when a goalie moved to stop his shot. He had a "feel" for how the game flowed, and how he could change that flow. Mario scored almost every time he had a clear look at the goal. On defense, Mario was rarely out of position. He knew how to get an angle

DID YOU KNOW?

Mario was a super-competitive kid, both on and off the ice. When he played Monopoly downstairs with his brothers, his father could always tell how the game was going. "If Mario lost, it would be as if a hurricane went through the basement," remembers Jean-Guy Lemieux.

ALAIN LEMIEUX
SALT LAKE GOLDEN EAGLES 1981/82

on an opponent, then use his momentum to check him off the puck. Almost every year, his team won the championship.

Around the age of 9, Mario's name began appearing in the local newspapers. By the time he was a teenager, every fan in Canada had heard of him, and NHL scouts could be spotted at most of his games. "I always got a lot of attention," Mario admits.

Part of the reason for this was that Alain, four years older, was already making headlines as a junior player. In 1979–1980, Alain scored 47 goals and had 95 assists for the Chicoutimi Sagueneens. He was chosen by the St. Louis Blues in the 4th round of the NHL draft and sent to the junior club in Trois Rivières, where he upped his goal total to 68.

No one who watched Mario doubted that one day he would be a great junior, too. Coaches described him as an alert and creative player. He never was caught by surprise; when he faced a new problem or situation, he invented a brilliant solution. Mario hated to lose, and he never gave up. He had everything you looked for in a young star, and then some.

When Mario posed for this picture as a boy, he never dreamed it would one day end up on a hockey card.

MARIO LEMIEUX

CENTER
PITTSBURGH PENGUINS

Sports Illustrated KiDS

2 MAJOR JUNIOR

"I don't worry about what people say. I know what my job is—to go out and score some big goals, make some plays."

MARIO LEMIEUX

Each spring, Canada's junior hockey leagues draft the country's most promising teenagers. Because Mario lived in the province of Quebec, he was ticketed for the Quebec Major Junior Hockey League (QMJHL). The worst QMJHL team during the 1981–1982 season was Laval, so it got the first pick. The Voisins chose Mario.

Mario had grown significantly as a teenager, and now stood well over 6 feet (183 centimeters) tall. This gave him extra reach, which is important both for stickhandling and on defense. Mario's size also gave him a long and quick first stride, which meant he

Mario prepares to fire a shot on goal in this trading card—one of the few showing him in a Laval uniform.

QHL Player Of The Week

If there's a rush of pro hockey scouts to Quebec in the near future it's because of the talents shown by a 16-year-old whiz with the Laval Voisins by the name of **Mario Lemieux**.

The youngster is the talk of the Quebec League, where he recently compiled a fantastic 14 scoring points in seven games to capture QHL Player of the Week honors.

The unbelievable thing about Lemieux is that in addition to being only 16, he's also 6-2 and weighs 191 and plays center — not defense — for Laval. Lemieux is naturally not draftable this season because of his age but you can bet he'll be in demand when his time comes for the NHL draft in 1984.

The youngster led the Voisins in scoring with 48 points in his first 34 games and he has been a big factor in Laval's continuing fight to keep ahead of Granby and Quebec in the race for a QHL playoff berth.

MARIO LEMIEUX
Laval Voisins

could move like lightning to a loose puck. He used these advantages to make his first junior season a good one. He scored 30 goals and set up teammates with assists 66 times.

With age came experience and a little extra muscle. Mario was a much better player in his second season with Laval. Defenders who had bodied him off the puck or shoved him while he tried to shoot found it much more difficult to move him during his second season. Sometimes it seemed as if Mario was moving *them* while he passed and shot. At other times the 17-year-old turned on the speed and swooshed past them like they were not even there. In 1982–1983, he finished with 84 goals and 100 assists in 66 games. Led by Mario and first-year defenseman Bobby Dollas, Laval finished atop the league and reached the championship game.

In Mario's third and final junior season, Laval added a tremendous young

Bobby Dollas gets the worst of a collision with Jay Wells of the Rangers. Dollas was the top defenseman on Mario's Laval team.

The Laval Voisins had two first-rate centers in 1983–1984. Mario and Vincent Damphousse (above) both became NHL All-Stars.

center named Vincent Damphousse. This gave the Voisins an excellent second line, which was bad news for opponents. When Mario skated to the bench for a breather, Damphousse would hop over the boards and continue the assault. The one-two punch enabled the team to blow most opponents right out of the rink. Mario seemed to get a goal or assist in just about every period. By mid-season he had 150 points (goals + assists).

Alas, all was not well in Mario's world. Despite his eye-popping scoring totals, many experts said he might not be the player he appeared to be. They believed the QMJHL was a cut below Canada's other junior leagues, and therefore his offensive numbers were a bit inflated. They also criticized Mario for not playing tight defense. What hurt Mario most was that people

DID YOU KNOW?

During Mario's second season with Laval, he met a girl named Nathalie Asselin. They dated for many years, then married in the 1990s.

were claiming that he was not tough enough, that he backed down from confrontations.

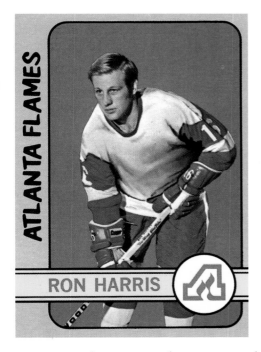

ATLANTA FLAMES

RON HARRIS

NHL scout Ron Harris had a feeling Mario's cards would soon be worth more than his. "He's the best I've seen at making plays and passing," he said of the junior superstar.

The truth of the matter was that opponents were always trying to "lure" Mario into taking stupid penalties, reasoning that this was the best way to keep him off the ice. Indeed, during his first two years in the juniors, a team's worst player could simply harass Mario until he retaliated. A couple of punches would be thrown, and both skaters would be sent to the penalty box. Obviously, this was a trade-off that other teams were all too happy to make—and one that drove Mario's coach crazy. By his third season, however, Mario had learned to hold his temper, and to accept the constant slashing and hacking as a kind of compliment. Yet now he was accused of being "soft!" One night, in a game against Shawinigan, Mario was being hooked and chopped until he decided enough was enough. He turned, dropped his gloves, and punched his opponent right in the nose. Mario skated to the penalty box, while the Shawinigan player lay sprawled on the ice.

Mario realized that the smart way to shut people up was to shatter records, not faces. He set his sights on the QMJHL's two famous scoring records. Thirteen years earlier his hero, Guy Lafleur, had tallied an amazing 130 goals for the Quebec Remparts. Three seasons after that Pierre Larouche of the Sorel Epiviers finished with 251

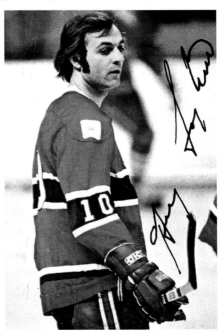

There was a time when Mario would have given anything for a Guy Lafleur autograph. After his third junior season, Mario's signature was in even greater demand.

Pierre Larouche, whose records Mario wiped from the books.

points. Spurred on by his critics—and the desire to be the top pick in the NHL draft—Mario finished the season with a flourish. He broke Lafleur's record with 133 goals and also amassed 149 assists, for a total of 282 points.

Just about every season during the 1970s and 1980s, one special player grabbed the spotlight in junior hockey. Obviously, in 1983–1984 that player was Mario. Yet as the NHL draft approached, it was becoming clear that Mario had gone a step beyond. He had few doubters by this time, and the NHL was ready to roll out the red carpet for him. Perhaps the best measure of the excitement Mario created that spring was that, for the first time in history, the pro draft would be a television "event." In years past, the selection process had been a closed-door affair. Now the Canadian Broadcast Company was airing it coast-to-coast in French and English.

There were many good players in the 1984 NHL draft, including Stephane Richer, Patrick Roy, Kirk Muller, Luc Robitaille, Kevin Hatcher, and Michal Pivonka. But there was little doubt whose name would be the first one called. Mario Lemieux was everybody's #1.

DID YOU KNOW?

The 10th center chosen after Mario in the 1984 NHL draft decided to play baseball instead of signing with the Los Angeles Kings. His name was Tom Glavine (right), and he went on to win two Cy Young awards with the Atlanta Braves.

JUNIOR STATS

Season	Team	Games	Goals	Assists	Points
1981–1982	Laval Voisins	64	30	66	96
1982–1983	Laval Voisins	66	84	100	184
1983–1984	Laval Voisins	70	133*	149*	282*
Total		**200**	**247**	**315**	**562**

* Led League

Canadian Junior Player of the Year *1983–1984*
All-Time QMJHL Scoring Record *1983–1984*
Mike Bossy Award (Top Prospect) *1983–-1984*

**Forward Luc Robitaille (below) was one of
several future NHL stars available in Mario's draft.**

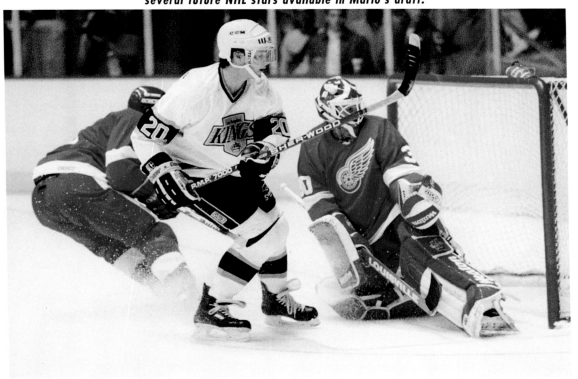

3 LEMIEUX DEBUT

"This is the greatest thing to happen to this franchise since its inception."

PITTSBURGH OWNER EDDIE DEBARTOLO

hen the 1983–1984 NHL season ended, the Pittsburgh Penguins had a league-worst record of 16–58–6 (16 wins, 58 losses, and 6 ties). Normally, there is little to cheer about when a team finishes with so few points. But in Pittsburgh that spring, there was plenty of excitement and controversy. In the final weeks, the Penguins were locked in "competition" with the New Jersey Devils to see who would end up with the league's worst record—and first pick in the draft.

Most Penguins fans were actually rooting for their team to do poorly. The team itself seemed to be doing its best to lose, too. In March, Pittsburgh traded away its best player, Randy Carlyle, and replaced starting goalie Roberto Romano with the inexperienced

Pittsburgh owner Eddie DeBartolo breathed a sigh of relief once the Penguins "won" the right to draft Mario.

Mario may have looked young, but he handled a tricky contract negotiation like an old pro.

Vincent Tremblay. The team finished with one less win than the Devils. When the Penguins clinched last place, general manager Eddie Johnston, coach Bob Berry, and owner Eddie DeBartolo beamed as if they had just won the Stanley Cup. Mario Lemieux was coming to Pittsburgh!

Mario's value to the franchise would be enormous. The Penguins had only four winning seasons in their entire history. They had almost no young talent, and they were in the same division as four tough teams: the New York Islanders, New York Rangers, Philadelphia Flyers, and Washington Capitals. It would take several years for the Penguins to rebuild, but in the meantime Mario would have time to develop his skills, and Pittsburgh fans would have someone to cheer for (and buy tickets to see).

The marketing of Mario began as soon as the regular season ended. The Penguins mailed elaborate brochures to fans that predicted how great he would be. The team's coaches and executives gave excited interviews to local reporters. A Pittsburgh television station ran commercials urging fans to tune in and witness their club pick Mario. Mario and his agent, Gus Badali, watched the commotion in Pittsburgh with great interest. Mario was already "making money" for the Penguins, so they reasoned that the team would offer him a generous contract.

Prior to the draft, the two sides held informal discussions. The contract DeBartolo had in mind, Badali learned, might not be as generous as he had hoped. Disappointed, he advised Mario to play "hardball" with the Penguins. At the draft, he refused to shake the general manager's hand when he was selected, and declined to be photographed in a Pittsburgh jersey. The fans were outraged. They thought Mario was a spoiled brat. They did not yet know about his famous stubborn streak. Indeed, when Mario made up his mind to do something, he became an immovable object.

Worried about the bad publicity he was receiving, Mario agreed to be interviewed by a Pittsburgh radio station so he could tell his side of the story. The city's fans tuned

Mario celebrates his first NHL goal, against the Boston Bruins.

in, and what they heard stunned them. This was not a whining, preening "prima donna." Mario was a relaxed, thoughtful, and honest 18-year-old whose self-confidence was sincere and refreshing. DeBartolo was listening, too. He knew that he had better sign Mario fast—or get run out of town! Two days later, the deal was done.

When the Penguins hit the ice for the 1984–1985 season, all eyes were on Mario. He wore number 66, which was Wayne Gretzky's number 99 turned upside down. Gretzky, who was at the height of his powers for the Edmonton Oilers, had turned *hockey* upside down. He passed and shot and skated like no one who had ever played the game. His goal and assist totals reached into the stratosphere. Though not particularly fast or strong, Gretzky glided through defenses like a sparrow flies through a porch railing. Sometimes he seemed to be playing a different sport than everyone else. There were those who said Mario had this same talent. Throughout the season, there were hints this was true. But without a good team around him, there was only so much Mario could do. The Penguins finished with a bad record and missed the playoffs once again.

In a season with few highlights, Mario's best moment may have been opening night in Pittsburgh. A sell-out crowd of 15,741 greeted him with a standing ovation as he took

DID YOU KNOW?

During Mario's rookie year, he lived with a Mount Lebanon family the team found for him. Tom and Nancy Matthews—and their three sons (ages 22, 21, and 19)—provided Mario with a great family atmosphere.

the opening faceoff. Eighteen seconds later, Mario found teammate Doug Shedden with a perfect pass, which Shedden tucked into the net. The Igloo (Pittsburgh's hockey arena) literally shook as fans stomped and screamed for their new superstar.

With each passing game, Mario learned a little more and got a better feel of what he could (and could not) do against veteran pros. He discovered that his stickhandling, skating, and passing were well above average for a big center. He also realized that, as one of the largest players in the NHL at 6 feet 4 inches (193 centimeters), he could plant himself in front of the goal, where he could score on rebounds and deflections. This combination made Mario very dangerous—if you

DID YOU KNOW?

With 43 goals and 57 assists, Mario became only the third rookie in NHL history to score 100 points.

set your defense to stop him one way he simply switched strategies and beat you another way. Still a teenager, he was already driving enemy coaches crazy. And he was only going to get bigger and better.

Mario's teammates were impressed with how he handled himself *between* games. Sometimes, a young superstar will slack off in practice, or act as if he is better than everyone else. No one skated harder, listened more, or asked more questions than Mario. He was also polite and generous to the people who worked for the team—from the janitors and ushers to the secretaries and front-office staff.

Mario was selected to play in the All-Star Game, and won the MVP award after scoring a pair of goals. At the end of the year he was everyone's choice to win the Calder Cup as the NHL's top first-year player. "One of my goals was to make Rookie of the Year," admits Mario. "I had to prove to Pittsburgh they didn't make a mistake by making me the first choice."

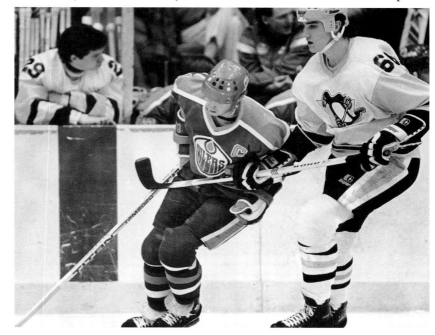

Mario manhandles Wayne Gretzky during their first meeting. Although Mario was much bigger than "The Great One," they had very similar skills.

*After an amazing rookie season, Mario made the cover of the
NHL's official season preview in 1985.*

MARIO THE MAGNIFICENT

4

"I'd like to be remembered as a winner, as somebody who helped his team to win a Stanley Cup."

MARIO LEMIEUX

Mario's first few NHL seasons proved he was a special player. Each year he found new ways to use his gigantic body, creative mind, and intense concentration in concert with his amazing hockey skills. Every time Mario took the ice, opponents only cared about one thing: stopping him. This meant that scoring opportunities did not come easy. Yet Mario was so good that when those chances *did* come, he rarely missed them. He tallied 141 points in 1985–1986, and topped 50 goals for the first time in 1986–1987.

Mario's big breakthrough occurred during the 1987–1988 season. He led the league in goals with 70, and in total points with 168. He won the Hart

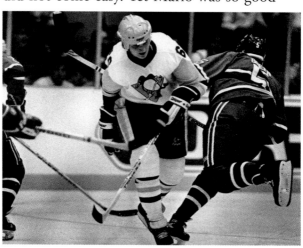

Mario makes his way through a maze of sticks and bodies during his second season. Every opponent had the same plan for beating the Penguins: Stop Mario!

21

Mario skates stride-for-stride with Wayne Gretzky. In 1988, he won the First-Team All-Star spot that Gretzky had occupied for seven seasons.

Trophy as the game's top player, and beat out Wayne Gretzky for First-Team honors on the NHL All-Star squad. Mario was not only the NHL's most dangerous offensive player, he had become the game's best penalty-killer, too. Whenever the Penguins were short-handed, Mario took over until his teammate returned to the ice. He would gain control of the puck and skate circles around opponents, as precious seconds ticked off the clock. Normally, teams press for goals when they get a power play. Against Pittsburgh, they were more worried about what *Mario* might do.

There was only one thing Mario could *not* do: Make the Penguins better. The team failed to win consistently during each of Mario's first four seasons, and not once did Pittsburgh advance to the postseason. Although some were saying Mario was now as good as Gretzky, Mario was the one watching the Stanley Cup playoffs each spring, and Gretzky was the one winning the cups. Whenever the Oilers needed a great play, "The Great One" rose to the occasion. Until Mario could prove himself like this, no one would take him seriously as a true superstar.

Of course, one reason Gretzky was

DID YOU KNOW?

In a 1988 game against the New Jersey Devils, Mario became the first player in NHL history to score five goals five different ways: At even strength, on a power play, short-handed, on a penalty shot, and into an empty net.

able to make his teammates better was that they were very good to begin with. Mark Messier, Glenn Anderson, Jari Kurri, Paul Coffey, and Grant Fuhr were all future Hall of Famers. When Mario looked around all he saw were inexperienced youngsters, over-the-hill veterans, and a lot of guys who would have been bench-warmers on other teams. Mario sometimes worried there was nothing he could do to help the Penguins reach the next level.

In the summer after his third season, Mario was selected to play in the Canada Cup tournament. Team Canada coach Mike Keenan decided to use Mario and Gretzky on the same line, and the results were magical. They worked together so well that opponents sometimes caught themselves watching the pair instead of defending against them. Mario scored 11 goals in nine games, including the tournament-winner against Russia. While they played and practiced together, Mario watched Gretzky closely. He was hoping to understand how he could be a better leader. Although it did not sink in immediately, the lesson Mario learned was that you have to break through your own limits before you can ask your teammates to do the same. "Every shift, Wayne tried to do the impossible," Mario remembers. "He gave me a lot of confidence in myself, and I brought it back to Pittsburgh."

Mario followed his sensational 1987–1988 campaign with an even better one in 1988–1989. More important, the Penguins had a new attitude. They were expecting to win games instead of trying not to lose them. This was a big step on the road to respectability. The team finished second in the division, with a 40–33–7 record. Mario led the league with 85 goals, 114 assists, and 199 points. These numbers rank among the best in the history of the sport.

Pittsburgh, in the playoffs for the first time since 1982, beat the New York Rangers in the opening round. Mario played brilliantly, especially on defense. The Penguins faced the Flyers in the second round, and seemed to take control of the series when Mario scored five times and had three assists (for a record 8 points) in Game 5. But the hard-nosed Flyers won the

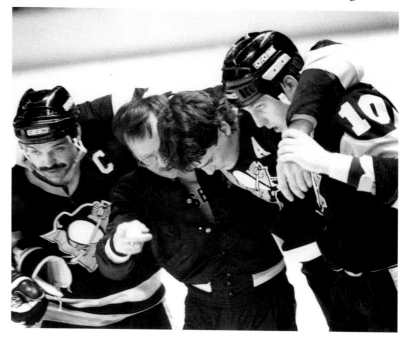

Mario is helped off the ice during a game against Washington. After 1989, he did not play a single year injury-free.

**Mario shows off the Hart
and Art Ross trophies he won in 1988.**

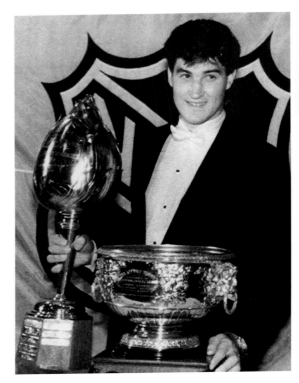

final two, including Game 7 at the Igloo, to end Pittsburgh's season.

Determined to take the Penguins deeper into the playoffs, Mario began the 1989–1990 season like a man on a mission. He scored a point in 46 consecutive games, and was on pace to threaten Gretzky's all-time scoring record. The Penguins were in a tough battle for the division crown, with just a handful of wins separating five teams. This was the kind of year Mario had fantasized about when he was a kid. Every day he woke up with a sense of purpose and excitement.

Then the nightmare began. During a game against the Rangers, Mario felt a horrible pain in his back. He left the ice and was examined by doctors, who determined that he had a herniated disk. One of the bones in his spine had popped out of place. It would take a month of rest before he could skate again. Mario watched helplessly as his teammates lost game after game, and sank lower and lower in the standings. With one game left, the Penguins needed to beat the Buffalo Sabres to secure the final berth in the playoffs. With his back still aching, Mario suited up and played in the season finale. His teammates watched in awe as he shook off the pain, scored a goal, and assisted on Pittsburgh's only other tally. But the Sabres scored three times to win, and Pittsburgh missed the playoffs. Things went from bad to worse a couple of months later, when Mario was forced to undergo surgery.

Mario kept in shape while his injury healed, and by the time training camp opened he felt strong enough to start skating again. However, during an exhibition game his back started aching again. A serious infection had developed near his fourth vertebra. Now it looked like he might have to miss the whole season. Worse, doctors were saying it was possible he might never be the same again.

5

FINALLY THE FINALS

"Hopefully, I can come back and have my best season."

MARIO LEMIEUX

Though big and strong, like Mario he possessed the speed and shiftiness of a much smaller player. Jagr was a confident stickhandler who looked to draw two defenders then pass off. He was also a deadly scorer with a fast, accurate wrist shot. Jagr was lefthanded, while

There was a silver lining in the dark cloud of Mario's injury. The Penguins had slipped far enough in the 1990 standings to get the fifth selection in the NHL draft. The team chose right wing Jaromir Jagr, a flashy 18-year-old from Czechoslovakia. Scouts said Jagr was the "mirror image" of Mario.

When the Penguins drafted Jaromir Jagr, Mario finally had a frontline forward with whom he could work.

25

Craig Patrick, the "architect" of the great Pittsburgh Penguin teams.

Mario was a righty. That was the major difference. The thought of these two playing on the same line was very exciting.

Another positive for Pittsburgh heading into the 1990–1991 season was that the team's decision-makers had a plan. A year earlier, Craig Patrick had been named General Manager, and following the 1989–1990 campaign he hired Scotty Bowman to help him with player decisions. Bowman had coached the great Montreal teams of the 1970s, and had been an announcer on *Hockey Night in Canada*. He knew the league's players, and understood what it took to build a champion. Patrick also hired Bob Johnson to coach the Penguins. Johnson had molded the Calgary Flames into Stanley Cup contenders several years earlier, and had a special talent for motivating players.

Despite what everyone else was saying, these three believed that the Penguins were quite close to having a championship team. When they learned that Mario's infection would keep him out for at least half the season, they looked for a way to make the most of his absence. Patrick, Bowman, and Johnson agreed that the best thing to do was to mold their remaining players into a confident, winning squad. Then when Mario returned, he would provide that final boost.

The Penguins had a good core of veterans to work with. Defenseman Paul Coffey, acquired from Edmonton in 1987, was a two-time winner of the Norris Trophy who skated and passed as well as any forward in the NHL. Bryan Trottier, who won four Stanley Cups with the Islanders, came to the Penguins as a free agent and provided

Pittsburgh's trade for Paul Coffey was front-page news.

experience and leadership in close games. Joe Mullen, a fearless and unselfish team player, came from Calgary, where he had starred for Coach Johnson years before. Goalie Tom Barrasso, who suffered through an injury-plagued 1989–1990 campaign, was back in good health. No one in the league handled the puck as well as Barrasso did—it was not unusual for him to get an assist by feeding a long pass to one of his forwards.

Besides Jagr, the team's younger stars included the little right wing, Mark Recchi, an intense and talented team player. He applied relentless pressure on opponents, often creating scoring chances where none seemed possible. Kevin Stevens created opportunities using the "freight-train" approach. The burly left wing skated right through opponents, often leaving a trail of spinning skaters in his path.

The Penguins picked up other valuable players after the season started. Ron Francis, one of the best passing centers in history, came from the Hartford Whalers in a trade for Rob Brown. The team hated to trade Brown, who was a dependable scorer. But when the Whalers threw in Ulf Samuelsson and Scott Young, they could not turn the deal down. Both were superior defensive players to the slow-footed Brown, and could skate rings around opponents. Larry Murphy, picked up in a trade with the

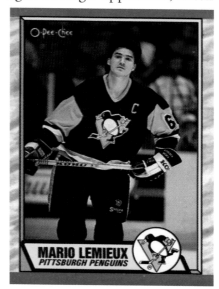

As this card shows, things were starting to look up for Mario and the Penguins.

Hard-working Joe Mullen (left) brought championship experience to the Penguins.

Minnesota North Stars, gave Pittsburgh a goal-scoring defenseman who could keep the pressure on opponents when Coffey was on the bench.

By mid-season, Coach Johnson had this group believing they could compete with anyone in the league. He tinkered with the team's chemistry and found combinations of players who worked especially well together. As the season's second half began, Pittsburgh was right in the thick of the playoff hunt. Meanwhile, Mario's back was gradually getting better. It frustrated him to miss so many games, but it was exciting to watch the team come together right before his eyes. He knew this club could win it all if he returned to the ice, and his teammates knew it, too.

At the end of January, Mario announced he was ready to play again. His first game came against the Quebec Nordiques, who battled the Penguins for 60 furious minutes. Mario made the difference, setting up three goals in a 6–5 victory. The mood in the locker room after the game was tremendous. Mario looked like he had never been hurt. With its confidence sky-high, the team roared through the rest of its schedule. Mario played in a total of 26 games and scored 45 points. The Penguins finished with 41 wins and captured the first division title in franchise history. Now it was time to go after the Stanley Cup.

Pittsburgh's first-round opponent was New Jersey, the team that had come within a loss of drafting Mario back in the 1980s. Since then the Devils had become a solid defensive team. They played the Penguins tough in this series, splitting the first four

Tom Barrasso turns back an enemy shot. He was also good at igniting the Pittsburgh attack.

games. In Game 5, fans at the Igloo expected an easy victory, but they left in shock as the visitors bottled up Mario and his teammates, 4–2. Pittsburgh won Game 6 to force a seventh game, but in the first period of the deciding contest, Mario drifted to the bench with back spasms. Confident they could win without their leader, the Penguins clamped down on the Devils and scored a 4–0 shutout to advance. Mario could not have been more proud of his teammates.

Mario covers up after a cross-check to the head. Though the Bruins resorted to thuggery, they could not keep him from dominating the 1991 Stanley Cup semifinals.

Knowing his star center would not be 100 percent, Coach Johnson suggested that Mario act as a decoy against the Washington Capitals in the second round of the play-offs. The plan was for Mario to lure Washington defenders out of position so that his linemates, Recchi and Stevens, would have more open ice. Although the Caps prevailed in the opener, the strategy proved effective. Behind the stellar goaltending of Barrasso, the Penguins swept the final four games of the series.

The Boston Bruins were now all that stood between the Penguins and their first trip to the Stanley Cup finals. The Bruins were wise to Pittsburgh's plan, and they won the first two games. Realizing he had to shake things up, Mario ignored the pain and seized control of the series.

DID YOU KNOW?

Mario finished the 1991 playoffs with 16 goals and 28 assists in 23 games. He was awarded the Conn Smythe Trophy as the postseason MVP.

He scored or assisted on almost every important goal the rest of the way, finishing with

> "He's unbelievably good now, and we don't know how good he will be."
>
> *GORDIE HOWE*

15 points. He also took the ice when the Penguins had to kill penalties, and dominated the action. The final four games were not even close, as Pittsburgh won them by a combined score of 20–7.

Pittsburgh fans were going wild. They would play the Minnesota North Stars for the Stanley Cup. The North Stars were a so-so club that had barely made the playoffs. They had been on a tremendous roll, upsetting the Chicago Blackhawks, St. Louis Blues, and the defending champion Edmonton Oilers. The team starred veterans Brian Bellows and Neal Broten, young Mike Modano, and goalie Jon Casey, but they lacked the depth and talent of the Penguins. Although victory seemed guaranteed, it would not come easily. Once again, the Penguins failed to nail down the opener, losing 5–4.

Mario scored a breathtaking goal in Game 2 to help win the game and tie the series, but he had to sit out Game 3 when his back was just too painful to play. Minnesota won, 3–1. Mario returned for Game 4 and scored three minutes into the contest as the Penguins went on to tie the series at 2–2. In the opening period of Game 5, Mario's line beat Casey four times. He scored one goal himself and set up Recchi on two others. The Penguins held on for a 6–4 win and a 3–2 series lead.

Mario could smell victory now. Two minutes into Game 6, Samuelsson netted a power-play goal to give the

Minnesota goalie Jon Casey sprawls in vain after Mario scores a short-handed goal.

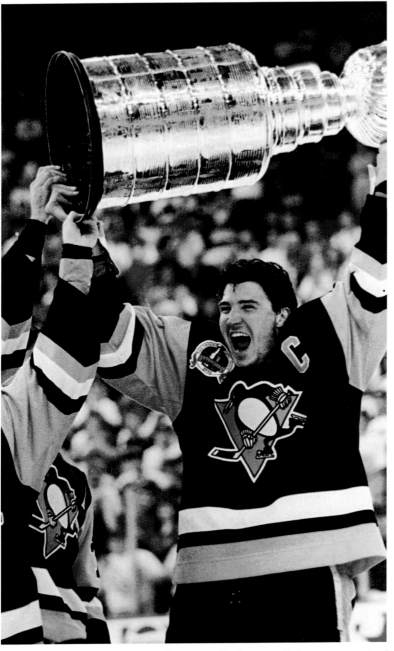

This is what it's all about. Mario hoists the Stanley Cup after beating the North Stars 8–0.

Penguins a 1–0 lead. The North Stars threatened to tie the game later in the period when Pittsburgh was forced to play short-handed. But Mario stole a pass and swooped in on Casey all alone. He faked once, twice, then a third time to draw the Minnesota goalie out of position and shoved the puck past him for a 2–0 lead. When Mullen scored a minute later, the North Stars simply gave up. Mario set up two more Pittsburgh goals in an 8–0 wipeout. The Penguins were Stanley Cup champs!

When the Penguins returned from Minneapolis, the city held a parade in their honor. More than 80,000 fans stood before the podium as each player was introduced to a deafening roar. The biggest cheer was reserved for Mario, whose comeback was being called one of the greatest in hockey history. "This cup is for you!" he shouted to the crowd.

ONE MORE TIME

6

"Bobby Orr was my hero growing up. But now Mario's my hero."

KEVIN STEVENS

Winning the Stanley Cup was the greatest feeling of Mario's life. As the summer began, he felt like nothing could stop the Penguins. They were on top of the world, and nothing could pull them down. That August, however, the team received sad news. While preparing to coach Team USA in the Canada Cup, Bob Johnson collapsed and was rushed to the hospital. Doctors removed several brain tumors during an emergency operation, but it was too late. He could no longer walk or talk. Johnson went home, where he died without ever getting a chance to say farewell to his players.

Would Kevin Stevens trade his own cards for Mario's? In a Pittsburgh minute!

KEVIN STEVENS
PENGUINS • LEFT WING/AILIER GAUCHE

The legendary Scotty Bowman.

Although Mario had received most of the headlines during the 1991 Stanley Cup, he knew that no one had more to do with the team's success than Coach Johnson. He feared that his dreams of a second championship would never come true. When the players gathered for training camp, they missed the upbeat attitude of the man they lovingly called "Badger Bob." They agreed to wear a special badger patch on their uniforms that year, and had Johnson's motto, *It's a Great Day for Hockey*, painted on the ice at the Igloo.

Luckily, the one man in hockey qualified to step in and coach a team in such disarray was sitting in the office down the hall from Craig Patrick. When the general manager asked Scotty Bowman to return to the bench, how could Bowman refuse? Bowman hated the daily grind of being an NHL coach, but he agreed to fill the job to honor his fallen friend.

Mario remembered from his days as a diehard Montreal fan that Bowman was a stern, no-nonsense coach who demanded nothing less than perfection. Any thoughts that he might have "mellowed" in his years away from the game were erased at the

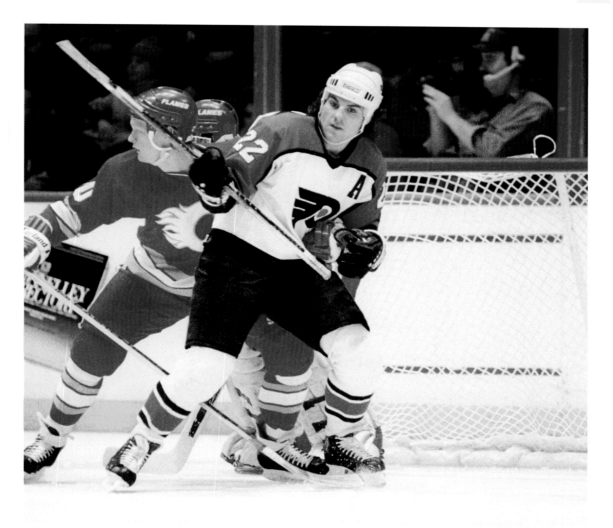

The late-season trade for Philadelphia's Rick Tocchet (above) energized the Penguins in 1992.

team's first practice. Bowman barked at his players constantly, and Mario could see they did not like it. Over the next few months, he tried to convince his teammates that Bowman was only trying to bring out the best in them. But by February the Penguins' record was .500, the players were getting down on themselves, and they were in jeopardy of missing the playoffs.

Mario was the lone bright spot during a difficult regular season. Despite missing 16 games with an aching back and sore shoulder, he managed to finish the year with 44

Mario clutches his wrist after a vicious slash by New York's Adam Graves.
Mario was fitted with a special cast and came back to beat the Rangers in the playoffs.

goals and 87 assists to lead the league with 131 points. The Penguins finally pulled together and played well down the stretch, finishing third in the division. The turning point came with less than a month to go. Looking for a way to energize the team, Patrick swapped Mark Recchi to the Philadelphia Flyers for sharpshooter Rick Tocchet, backup goalie Ken Wregget, and Kjel Samuelsson, an enormous defenseman.

Although the team looked solid for the playoffs, Mario was not 100 percent. He was unable to play in Pittsburgh's first postseason game against the Washington Capitals because of his shoulder. The Caps won 3–1, then took the next game by a score of 6–2. The teams split the next two contests, which put Pittsburgh behind 3 games to 1. With the Penguins on the brink of elimination, Mario dug down deep and, as always, found a little extra. He dominated the next three games as only he could, leading Pittsburgh to the second round and finishing with 7 goals and 10 assists. "We were beaten by one man," said Terry Murray, the dejected coach of the Caps. And that man was Mario.

The New York Rangers, who owned the NHL's best record, were not about to let this happen to them. They assigned forward Adam Graves to shadow Mario—

wherever he went, Graves was to stay right next to him. Although this kept Mario from scoring in Game 1, he did manage to get two assists, and the Penguins won, 4–2. In Game 2, Graves delivered a vicious slash that broke Mario's left wrist. The Rangers won, Graves was suspended, and the Penguins were left without their best player.

Now it was time for Coach Bowman's harsh discipline and grueling practices to pay off. Instead of folding, the entire team picked it up and played brilliantly. With the series knotted at two games apiece, the Penguins went into Madison Square Garden and pulled out a stirring 3–2 win. Yearning to play, Mario was fitted with a special cast and got back into action for Game 6. His presence confounded the New Yorkers and inspired his teammates to a 5–1 win.

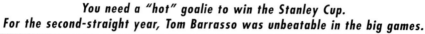

You need a "hot" goalie to win the Stanley Cup.
For the second-straight year, Tom Barrasso was unbeatable in the big games.

The Penguins had a lot to be happy about. Their Stanley Cup was a great ending to a difficult year.

From there, the rest was easy. Brimming with confidence, Pittsburgh faced Boston in the conference finals for the second straight year. This time they swept the Bruins to advance to the finals against the Chicago Blackhawks. Mario led the Penguins to another sweep, with five goals in four games. For the second-straight year he was awarded the Conn Smythe Trophy as playoff MVP. Despite sitting out six games, he led all players in the postseason with 34 points.

Mario circles the ice with the Stanley Cup—his second in two seasons.

7 GREATEST CHALLENGE

"My health is more important than playing hockey."

MARIO LEMIEUX

When the 1992–1993 season opened, there was not a Pittsburgh fan alive who doubted that the Penguins were on the verge of creating a hockey dynasty. The team had steady goaltending, an excellent defense, a good mix of veterans and youngsters, a terrific coach, the game's best up-and-coming player in Jaromir Jagr, and the best player on the planet, *period*, in Mario Lemieux.

"Super Mario," as he was now known throughout the sports world, lived up to his nickname. He scored at least one goal in each of his first dozen games, and reached the 100-point level in December. Wayne Gretzky's record of 215 points in a season seemed well within Mario's reach. The Penguins were humming along, way ahead in their division, looking unstoppable.

Then came a startling discovery. While Mario was undergoing routine treatment on his back, doctors saw something alarming. They did some tests and determined that he

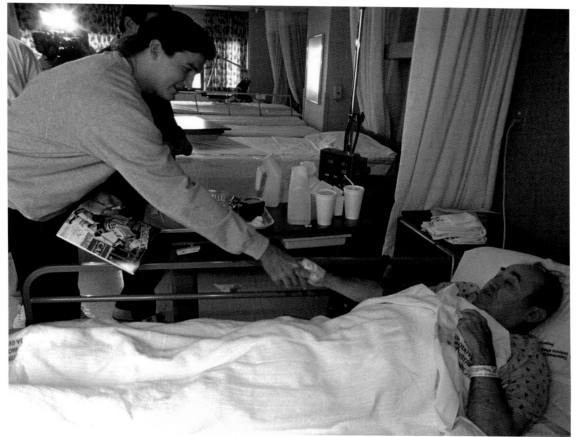

Mario was no stranger to Pittsburgh hospitals. Before being diagnosed with cancer, he liked to lift patients' spirits with surprise visits.

had cancer. Mario was devastated. "I went back home that day and I could hardly drive because of all the tears," he recalls. "I cried all day. It's scary any time you hear the word *cancer*. That certainly was the toughest day of my life."

Mario had Hodgkin's Disease, a type of cancer that attacks the lymph nodes. Luckily, it was caught in time. He was told that it probably was curable, and that the treatment would take a couple of months. Mario started radiation therapy, and responded so well that he was back practicing by March. Throughout the ordeal, he remained upbeat and treated it like any other challenge. "I'm a very positive person by nature," Mario says. "The cancer and everything were just something I had to go through and then forget about."

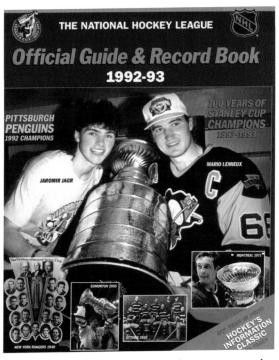

Mario and Jaromir Jagr smile from the cover of the NHL Guide. The 1992–1993 season would not be a happy one, however.

Needless to say, Mario's teammates were thrilled to see him. After losing Coach Johnson, some had feared that Mario was dying, too, and that they were not being told. For six weeks, the Penguins had played distracted, lackluster hockey, not knowing whether their leader would come back or not.

When Mario felt he was ready to play again, he walked into the locker room before a game against the Flyers and pulled on his uniform. His teammates were bewildered, and also a little nervous. They were concerned he was coming back too soon.

When Mario took the ice that evening, he got a long, standing ovation—both from the crowd, and the Philadelphia Flyers. He scored a goal that night, but the Penguins lost, 5–4.

Mario put his teammates' fears to rest by playing as if he had never taken a day off. He seemed to score a goal or two almost every night. The Penguins rallied around Mario and played great hockey, too. Beginning on March 9, Pittsburgh won 17 straight games. During this streak, Mario was on fire. He had 27 goals and 24 assists. The Penguins finished the year 56–21–7—by far the best record in team history. And despite missing 24 games, Mario actually won the NHL scoring championship again, edging Pat LaFontaine by 12 points. "I thought about it even during radiation," he says of the scoring title. "I was determined to come back and regain the lead."

The Penguins made quick work of the New Jersey Devils in the first round of the playoffs, and planned to do the

DID YOU KNOW?

Mario picked a good season to miss. The 1994–1995 schedule was cut to 48 games after a labor dispute delayed the opening of the season.

same against the New York Islanders in the second round. But Pittsburgh ran into the most dangerous obstacle in playoff hockey: a hot goalie. New York's Glenn Healey, who won just 22 games during the year, made big saves when he had to, and the Islanders edged the Penguins in seven wild games.

Mario was disappointed with his team's unexpected exit from the postseason, but thankful for his miraculous recovery. He began to look at hockey and his life in a different way. He had married his longtime girlfriend, Nathalie, and they had their first child, Lauren, that summer. Even when doctors recommended more back surgery, Mario took it in stride. By this time, he assumed that he would simply work his way into shape and pick up right where he left off.

Unfortunately, this was not the case anymore. Although the operation went well, Mario's back did not heal quickly. He missed the beginning of the 1993–1994 season, and was in and out of the lineup all year. During one stretch he missed 38 games in a

row, and he never played a day without pain. The Penguins, who by this time were used to skating without Mario, won their division anyway. But when the playoffs rolled around, they just were not ready. The Capitals beat them in five games.

That summer, for the first time in his life, Mario wondered whether he wanted to play hockey again. He no longer had the strength and stamina he once did, and, to make matters worse, the referees seemed to be letting defenses get away with more slashing and hooking than ever before. Competing under these conditions was not much fun. Ravaged by cancer and worn down by thousands of hours battling on the ice, his body was giving out. In August, Mario announced that he was going to take a year off.

Mario follows Jaromir Jagr out of the locker room during the 1993 playoffs. Little did they realize how hard a "three-peat" would be.

SIMPLY SUPER

There's more to Mario than meets the eye. Here's a portrait of the "Magnificent One" painted in the words of his hockey peers.

"He's the only guy who can make the puck disappear for a second. *Here's the puck now— oops, where is it? Oh, he still has it.*"

PAUL KARIYA (RIGHT-TOP)

"Right now, he's the best there is by far."

TERRY MURRAY, WASHINGTON COACH

"If you go at Mario like a madman, he'll make you look like a complete idiot."

DEFENSEMAN RAY BORQUE (RIGHT-CENTER)

"He proved he's the best player in the world."

TEAMMATE TROY LONEY

"Even at 10 years old, you saw the confidence. Mario was the best at every age, and he knew it. He thought like a veteran."

MARC BERGEVIN, CHILDHOOD FRIEND AND NHL PLAYER (RIGHT-BOTTOM)

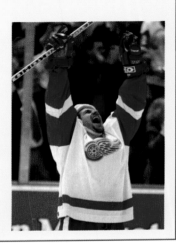

"Like Gretzky, he does miracles with the puck."

—CLAUDE CARRIER, QMJHL EXEC

"He can make passes that no one else can see, make plays like nobody else."

JAROMIR JAGR (RIGHT-TOP)

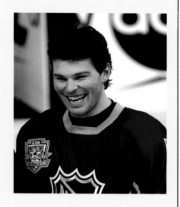

"You never know what to expect. His face is so calm. He shows no sign of stress or anything. A lot of goaltenders get nervous when he's coming at them with that face. It's as if he's saying, *No problem. Relax. I'm just going to beat you now. It's not going to hurt a bit.*"

GOALIE DOMINIC ROUSSEL

"There wasn't going to be hockey in Pittsburgh anymore if not for Mario. And we wouldn't have won the Cup without him."

TOM BARRASSO (RIGHT-CENTER)

COMING BACK FOR MORE

8

"If you have a second chance to do something you love, you appreciate it more."

MARIO LEMIEUX

Mario made some important decisions during his year away from hockey. He realized that his family and his health now came before his career. After his second daughter, Stephanie, was born in 1994, he tried to imagine how sad it would be if he could not pick up his kids and play with them. In years past, he might have put his fears away and returned to hockey full of fire. But Mario was starting to think like an adult. "Any time you go through something like I did, you have to take a step back," he says of his transformation. "It makes you grow up a lot faster."

Although it was tempting to retire for good, Mario decided to return to the NHL—but on his own terms. He would no longer put up with clinging, clawing defensemen. If the referees refused to call penalties, then he would attack the net in a different way. And when his back was bothering him, he would not feel guilty about sitting out. Mario's goal was to win another Stanley Cup, so he was not going to kill himself in the regular season. He wanted to be well rested for the playoffs.

Dedication, concentration, and talent made Mario a great hockey player. But it was another quality that helped him fight his disease. "If you don't have courage," he says, "you're not going to beat Hodgkin's Disease."

Mario scores on John Vanbiesbrouck in the 1996 NHL playoffs.
The Panthers (and the flu) held Mario in check, and Pittsburgh ended up losing the series.

As the NHL learned during the 1995–1996 campaign, Mario Lemieux playing at three-quarters speed was still better than anyone else in the league. He suited up for 70 of Pittsburgh's 82 games, and led all players with 69 goals and 92 assists. The Penguins ended the year with a 49–29–4 record and finished first in their division for the fourth time in six seasons. In the playoffs, the Penguins won their first two series with ease before encountering the league's hottest defense, which belonged to the Florida

Talk about a comeback! Not only did Mario beat cancer — he returned to win the 1996 Hart Trophy as the NHL's MVP.

Panthers. The underdog Panthers, led by goalie John Vanbiesbrouck, shut down the Pittsburgh attack. Mario tried his best to get the Penguins going, but a bout with the flu kept him from playing his best and once again the team was denied a trip to the Stanley Cup finals.

The following fall, Mario announced that he would play one more season and then retire. Sadly, what should have been a glorious farewell tour turned out to be one of the most anxiety-filled years of his life. In January of 1997, Mario discovered a lump on his neck. He panicked, thinking his cancer had returned. Tests proved this was not so, but Mario was now constantly worried about his health.

Two months later, Nathalie delivered their third child prematurely. Little Austin, weighing just two pounds, struggled to stay alive. Understandably, Mario had a hard time concentrating on hockey. Yet he still led the league in scoring, with 50 goals and 72 assists. Based on these numbers, many fans thought Mario would keep playing—after all, why quit when you are on top? The way *he* saw it, there was no better time to quit. At an April banquet, Mario confirmed that he would hang up his skates after the playoffs.

Mario waves to the crowd in his final home game of the 1996–1997 season. He retired after leading the NHL in scoring again.

The Penguins really wanted to give their leader one more Stanley Cup before he left, but the talent was no longer there. The Philadelphia Flyers took the first three games of their opening-round series, all but eliminating the Penguins. In Game 4, which was likely to be Mario's last appearance in Pittsburgh, he scored on a breakaway. The fans rose to their feet, and for several minutes the Igloo trembled as they roared their appreciation. It was the longest, loudest, most loving moment in his career. Mario started to cry. "I was just expressing my feelings toward the crowd, how I feel about the fans," he remembers. "It was a great moment. It was something I'll remember for a long time."

Mario embraces fellow superstar Eric Lindros after his last NHL game.

9 OWNER'S BOX

"I'm happy with my place in history."

MARIO LEMIEUX

ife without hockey suited Mario Lemieux. He spent time with his wife and children, sharpened his golf game, and really relaxed for the first time. He missed the camaraderie of the locker room and the adrenaline-rush of the playoffs, but knew he had nothing left to prove on the ice. Mario had retired with more than 600 goals, and averaged more goals per game than anyone in history. He had won the Hart Trophy three times as league MVP, the Art Ross Trophy as top scorer six times, and owned the all-time records for most overtime

goals and short-handed goals. As soon as Mario retired, the NHL waived its normal three-year waiting period and immediately inducted him into the Hall of Fame.

Although he was no longer part of the team, Mario followed the Penguins closely. He wanted them to do well—partly because he still had friends on the club, and partly

Mario poses with Wayne Gretzky and Michael Jordan at his charity golf tournament. Mario's golf game improved dramatically after he quit hockey.

Mario faces the press after taking control of the ailing Pittsburgh Penguins.

because he was still owed a lot of money. Mario had agreed to let Pittsburgh spread his salary out over many years so that the team could afford to sign other players right away.

After Mario retired attendance dropped, and the team found itself in financial trouble. If the Penguins folded, he stood to lose millions. Mario saw a way to protect his money and boost the team's fortunes at the same time. He had always been interested in owning a hockey team, and here was a golden opportunity. Using the money owed to him as "payment," he took control of the Penguins prior to the 1999–2000 season. For the second time in 15 years, Mario would attempt to save hockey in Pittsburgh.

Everyone in the organization was thrilled to have Mario back. They knew him to be a kind and respectful man, but one who would accept nothing less than everyone's

PRO HIGHLIGHTS

Hart Trophy (League MVP)	1987–1988, 1992–1993, 1995–1996
Conn Smythe Trophy (Playoff MVP)	1990–1991, 1991–1992
Art Ross Trophy (Scoring Leader)	1987–1988, 1988–1989, 1991–1992, 1992–1993, 1995–1996, 1996–1997
Lester Pearson Award (MVP as selected by players)	1985–1986, 987–1988, 1992–1993, 1995–1996
Calder Memorial Trophy (Rookie of the Year)	1984–1985
NHL First-Team All-Star	1987–1988, 1988–1989, 1992–1993, 1995–1996, 1996–1997
Stanley Cup Champion	1990–1991, 1991–1992
All-Star MVP	1985, 1988, 1990
Hall of Fame	1997
Olympic Gold Medalist	2002

best effort. Almost overnight, the Penguins regained their old pride. Mario proved he was a take-charge owner when he announced that the team could no longer afford its high-priced stars, and would begin replacing them with talented youngsters who were hungry to win. Normally, fans stop buying tickets when they hear this. But since the news was coming from Mario, ticket sales actually increased, and the crowds got louder and more enthusiastic. The Penguins rewarded their new boss by making the playoffs in 2000. They wiped out the hated Capitals in the first round before falling to Philadelphia in a dramatic, hard-fought series.

Mario enjoyed being an owner. He especially liked the fact that he could influence league matters in ways he could not as a player. Mario spearheaded a drive to "clean up" the NHL by discouraging violence and making sure referees whistled players for the kinds of infractions that had driven him from the sport. It was difficult for league officials and fellows owners to ignore him now that he was an "insider," and no one questioned his commitment. "I'm willing to do whatever it takes to help make our game better," Mario says. "I think this should be a concern to all of us—the league, the Players Association, and the fans. We want our sport to continue to grow, but it can't unless the violence stops growing first."

Moments like these convinced Mario the time was right for retirement.
As an owner, he pressured the league to crack down on dirty play.

10 SKATING INTO HISTORY

"My goal is to be better than I was in 1997."

MARIO LEMIEUX

A s others around the league joined Mario in his battle to clean up the game, the NHL finally began to listen. Going into the 2000–2001 season, in fact, new rules were passed to cut down on the clutching, grabbing, and holding that Mario believed was ruining hockey. The idea was to return to a time when stickhandling, passing, skating, and shooting won games—much like the time when Mario first broke into the league. This focus on artistry might disappoint some of the more bloodthirsty fans, but it would attract many more new fans to NHL arenas.

The tighter rules certainly pleased Jaromir Jagr. In the three years after Mario retired, he had become the star of the Penguins, and was considered by many to be the finest player in the league.

"Mario is pumped. He's pushing himself. He's got the itch to play again."

JAROMIR JAGR

Mario is all smiles at a December 2000 news conference, as he announces his return to the NHL. He was back in action on the 27th.

Mario was glad his friend had time to enjoy the spotlight, and when Jagr spoke with excitement about the big season he was expecting to have, Mario got a little excited, too. When the two legends skated together for an ESPN video in the fall of 2000, Mario started to really miss hockey for the first time.

Not long after that, Mario started thinking about a comeback. There were three things that made him want to do it. First, he was only 35, and still in good shape. Second, he was sure the referees would prevent opponents from brutalizing him. And third, he wanted Austin to see him play. The little guy had hovered at the brink of death for days after he was born, then made an amazing comeback. Mario owed it to him to make one himself.

Mario began running, lifting weights, doing quickness drills, and getting massages to loosen up his back. He asked equipment manager Steve Latin to order a large shipment of his favorite sticks. He held private practices with ex-NHL players and a former college goalie. In December, certain that he could perform at a level that met even *his* high standards, Mario announced his plan to rejoin the Penguins. He decided to make his return on December 27, a home game against the Toronto Maple Leafs.

Mario peels off his equipment after his first practice.
It felt great to be out there with the guys again.

The fan response was incredible. Within two days the Penguins had sold more than 10,000 tickets. Around the league, people were buying seats for their team's next game against the Penguins. Sales of Mario's number 66 jersey went through the roof. Almost overnight, the face of hockey had changed.

Mario creates havoc in front of the net during his first game back.

While the press responded to news of the comeback with excitement and amazement, hockey people hardly seemed surprised. "It's about two years overdue," joked Wayne Gretzky. "Mario could lace up his skates today and not miss a beat."

"This isn't great for the rest of us in the Eastern Conference," added Sabres coach Lindy Ruff, "but it's great for the game. I'd pay to see Mario play any day."

A sold-out crowd witnessed Mario's return in Pittsburgh. They cheered him from pregame warm-ups until the first period began. Thirty-three seconds into the game Mario scooped up a loose puck behind the Toronto net and fired a perfect pass to Jagr,

Mario never realized how much he missed the cheers until he "un-retired."

who flicked it past goalie Curtis Joseph. Mario scored a goal himself late in the game and assisted on another to lead Pittsburgh to a 5–0 win. It was an extraordinary performance, to say the least. Of course, "I didn't come back to be ordinary," Mario points out.

Mario's first night back was merely a preview of things to come. He was awesome, with 35 goals and 41 assists in just 43 games. Despite starting the season just before the midway point, Mario finished among the league leaders in power-play goals (16) and scoring percentage (20.5%), and was voted to the league's Second-Team All-Star squad. Before he joined them, the Penguins were 15–15–6. With Mario on the team, their record was 27–16–3.

Pro Stats

Season	Team	Games	Goals	Assists	Points
1984–1985	Penguins	73	43	57	100
1985–1986	Penguins	79	48	93	141
1986–1987	Penguins	63	54	53	107
1987–1988	Penguins	77	70*	98	168*
1988–1989	Penguins	76	85*	114*	199*
1989–1990	Penguins	59	45	78	123
1990–1991	Penguins	26	19	26	45
1991–1992	Penguins	64	44	87	131*
1992–1993	Penguins	60	69	91	160*
1993–1994	Penguins	22	17	20	37
1994–1995	Penguins	DID NOT PLAY			
1995–1996	Penguins	70	69	92	161*
1996–1997	Penguins	76	50	72	121*
1997–1998	Penguins	DID NOT PLAY			
1998–1999	Penguins	DID NOT PLAY			
1999–2000	Penguins	DID NOT PLAY			
2000–2001	Penguins	43	35	41	76
TOTAL		788	648	922	1,570

* Led NHL or tied for lead

More thrills followed in the playoffs. Mario led all scorers with four goals and three assists as Pittsburgh eliminated the Capitals in the first round, 4 games to 2. In the second round, the Buffalo Sabres won three of the first four games before Mario led the Penguins back. In Game 6, he saved his team from elimination with a game-tying goal late in the third period (Pittsburgh won in overtime). The Penguins then took Game 7 in overtime. Unfortunately for Mario, the team's magical ride finally ended against the New Jersey Devils in the conference finals, 4 games to 1.

Though asked often to reflect upon his return to hockey, Mario almost always prefers to look forward instead. He had so much fun in 2001 that he would like to play several more years as long as he remains healthy. "I had a lot of great moments in the early 1990s," he says. "But to be back and have a chance to play one more time has been great, especially with me playing well and the team playing well."

Mario and Jaromir Jagr celebrate Jagr's 1,000th career point. The Czech superstar won the 2001 scoring title with Mario at his side.

How incredible was his comeback? Many great players have returned from retirement for a "last hurrah," and a few have shown flashes of their former brilliance. But no one in any sport has done what Mario did. After three years away, he took a so-so team and got it playing consistent .600 hockey. If you project Mario's stats over an entire season, he would have finished with 66 goals and 78 assists—which means he would have won the scoring championship by more than 20 points!

Old-timer Igor Larionov, who has been facing off against the world's top players since 1977, calls Mario "the bright color of the game." The Russian star brings an interesting perspective to Mario's comeback. "People want to see a Monet, a Rembrandt at work," Larionov explains. "Whenever he's on the ice, he's capable of producing a masterpiece."

Whether Mario plays a few more years, a few more months, or just wakes up one morning and decides to hang up his skates, nothing can diminish what he has accomplished during this dramatic return—as well as all the others. Something unique and powerful burns deep within him, something that makes him yearn to prove himself again and again and again. The bigger the mountain Mario must climb, the more personal the obstacle, the harder he will strive to succeed.

Sports fans like to think that the best measure of an athlete lies somewhere in his statistics. For the most part, this is true. But every so often someone comes along whose numbers only hint at what he has meant to his fans, his teammates, and his sport. In the case of Mario Lemieux, the awesome stats are just the beginning of a story that seems to have an endless amount of inspirational twists, turns, and surprises. Where the story ends is anyone's guess ... with Mario, every time you close the book, the cover seems to pop open again!

Mario celebrates the only honor that had eluded him in his career: Olympic gold.
He helped Team Canada beat the United States 5–2 in the final at Salt Lake City in 2002.

INDEX

PAGE NUMBERS IN ITALICS REFER TO ILLUSTRATIONS.